EXPOSITORY OUTLINES
ON THE
LIFE OF CHRIST

EXPOSITORY OUTLINES
ON THE
LIFE OF CHRIST

Croft M. Pentz

BAKER BOOK HOUSE
Grand Rapids, Michigan

CONTENTS

1 THE WISE MEN VISIT JESUS

Matthew 2:1-23

I. **The wonder—vv. 1-8**
Though Christ's birth had been promised as long ago as Genesis 3:15, many were surprised when it occurred. Others were filled with doubt.
   A. People—vv. 1-2. Herod ruled Jerusalem for thirty-three years. The wise men asked, "Where is He?"
   B. Problem—v. 3. Herod was afraid that Jesus would become a leader. Herod had even killed some of his own sons because of jealousy.
   C. Plot—vv. 4-8. Herod didn't want to worship Jesus—he wanted to kill Him. He feared that Christ might take over his kingdom.

II. **The worship—vv. 9-11**
   A. Guidance—vv. 9-10. God led the wise men to Bethlehem. He will always lead, if man desires to follow (Prov. 3:5-6).
   B. Gifts—v. 11. Gold—tribute to a king. Frankincense—worship to God. Myrrh—bitter sufferings.
   C. Gifts we give to Christ:
      1. Self (Rom. 12:1-2; Matt. 6:33).
      2. Substance. Our time, talent, and tithes.
      3. Service. Working for and serving Him (Mark 16:15; John 15:16).

III. **The warning—vv. 12-15**
   A. Plan—vv. 12-13. God told them to go to Egypt to escape Herod, who had plans of killing Christ.
   B. Purpose—v. 14. Mary and Joseph didn't understand, but they knew God had a plan and purpose in all things.
   C. Prophecies—v. 15. A fulfilment of Hosea 11:1. God sees the future and leads accordingly.

IV. **The wrong—vv. 16-23**
   A. Plan—v. 16. In an effort to destroy Christ, Herod ordered all children, two years old and under be killed.
   B. Prophecy—vv. 17-18. Fulfilment of Jeremiah 31:15. The fulfilled prophecies of the Old Testament in the New prove the Bible.
   C. Protection—vv. 19-23. After the Herod who threatened ·Christ's life had died; Joseph, Mary, and Jesus returned to Nazareth. (There were many men in the Bible by the name of Herod.)

Man may seek to destroy God's work, but God permits man to go only so far. How foolish of man to think he can destroy God's work. Despite all the examples of man's failure in opposing God, there are still those who feel, as Herod did, that they can destroy God and His work.

2 CHRIST CALLS PETER AND ANDREW

Matthew 4:12-25

I. The Savior comes—vv. 12-16
   A. Prison—v. 12. Christ, hearing of John's imprisonment, departed and went into Galilee. (See also Matthew 14:1-12.)
   B. Places—vv. 13-15. The cities and the areas which Christ came into are named. Keep in mind that in Christ's day people had to walk everywhere they went.
   C. Prophecy—v. 16. Christ is the Light spoken of in Isaiah 9:2. Christ said He is the Light of the World.

II. The Savior calls—vv. 17-22
   A. The message—v. 17. Christ preached repentance. The word *repent* means a change of heart; a change in your way of living. It means to stop sinning and start living right.
   B. The men—v. 18. Christ saw Peter and Andrew fishing. Fishing was the occupation of many men in those days.
   C. The making—v. 19. Christ said, "Follow me, and I will make you fishers of men." Two important words: *follow* and *make*. If we follow Christ, He will make us what He wants us to be. We should permit Christ to work in us and with us. We should be like clay in Christ's hands, allowing Him to mold us in the way He wants us to live.
   D. The method—vv. 20-22. Note that they "straightway" or *immediately* followed the Lord. They did not take time to count the cost, or state any reservations—they followed. Later, as recorded in verse 21, He called others and they followed Him.

III. The Savior's concern—vv. 23-25
   A. The ministry—v. 23. The ministry of Christ was threefold:
      1. Teaching—He taught men about God, and how to live for God.
      2. Preaching—He preached the gospel.
      3. Healing—He healed all types of sickness.
   B. The miracles—v. 24. He healed all types of sickness:
      1. Divers diseases—all types of sickness.
      2. Torments—those with deep suffering and pain.
      3. Possessed with devils—the demon possessed.
      4. Lunatics—the insane.
      5. Palsied—those who were paralyzed.
   C. The multitudes—v. 25. Great crowds followed Him everywhere.

3 AN EXAMPLE OF FAITH

Matthew 8:1-13

I. The problem—vv. 1-6
  A. The cleansing—vv. 1-4. A leper asked for healing. Note Jesus' words, "I will." The leper was healed.
  B. The city—v. 5. Capernaum was about eighty miles north of Jerusalem.
  C. The centurion—v. 5. The word *centurion* designates a captain in charge of about a hundred men in the Roman army.
  D. The call—v. 6. He called on Jesus for help. Even though all others fail to help, Christ is near to deliver us.

II. The promise—vv. 7-9
  A. Sure promise—v. 7. See the words of Jesus, "I will come and heal him."
  B. Simple plan—v. 8. The centurion said, "You don't have to come to my house and touch the servant—just speak the word and he will be healed." This is the simple faith Christ wants from us.
  C. Simple person—v. 9. He was a great person, but had childlike faith . . . the kind God requires.

III. The power—vv. 10-12
  A. Pleasing faith—v. 10. God does not ask that we understand all things; He asks only that we believe. Such faith pleases God.
  B. Pardoning faith—v. 11. The Jews thought the promises of God were for them alone, but the gospel is for all people. (Note the word *whosoever* in John 3:16; Rom. 10:13.)
  C. Punishment without faith—v. 12. Whether a person be a Jew, Catholic, or Protestant, if he fails to accept Christ as his Savior, he will be lost (John 3:1-8).
The Bible has much to say about faith. Faith is not only in the head, but is in the heart (Rom. 10:9-10).

IV. The perfection—v. 13
  A. Command of faith—"Go thy way." The centurion went, believing without seeing the results. Anyone can believe when they see, but real faith believes before it sees.
  B. Completion of faith—"And his servant was healed in the self-same hour." Jesus tells of the power of this faith (Matt. 17:20). Different types of faith are saving faith, keeping faith, healing faith, active faith, and overcoming faith.

4 CHRIST GIVES LIFE

Matthew 9:1-26

I. The Savior—vv. 1-8
  A. Pardon—vv. 1-2. A man, sick with palsy, was brought to Christ. Christ not only forgives, but heals. Note these four magic words, "Be of good cheer."
  B. Problem—v. 3. The scribes were critical of Christ, accusing Him of blasphemy.
  C. Power—vv. 4-6. Jesus always had an answer for His critics. He showed that the Son of God had power to forgive sin. The Jews were blind to the fact that Jesus was God in the form of man. Since He is equal to God in power, He has power to forgive sin.
  D. Praise—vv. 7-8. When the people saw the work of God, they joined in praising God.

II. The sinners—vv. 9-17
  A. Call—v. 9. Christ called Matthew. Matthew arose and followed. He made no demands, asked no questions, and made no excuses. When God calls, we should follow as Matthew did.
  B. Company—v. 10. Jesus ate with the publicans. The publicans were tax collectors of whom many were dishonest, yet Christ took time to be with them. He didn't approve of their sin, but He loved their souls.
  C. Criticism—v. 11. Christ was criticized by the Pharisees for eating with sinners. As Christians, we should hate sin, but love the soul of the sinners.
  D. Conversion—vv. 12-14. Christ came to seek and save men lost in sin. He did not come to criticize the world—He came to convert the world.
  E. Comparison—vv. 15-17. Christ spoke of His return. He compared the Jewish religion to old "patched up" garments.

III. The sickness—vv. 18-26
  A. Death—v. 18. A ruler (rabbi) came, telling that his daughter had died. This man had faith that if Christ came and touched her, she would live again.
  B. Desire—vv. 19-22. The woman with a sickness (bleeding) for twelve years, desired to touch Jesus. If she only could touch Jesus, she had faith that she would be healed.
  C. Deliverance—vv. 23-26. The young girl, who had died (v. 18), was brought back to life by Christ. His fame spread throughout the land.

5 THE HELPFUL CHRIST

Matthew 9:27-38

I. The power—vv. 27-31
    A. People—v. 27. Two blind men cried out to Christ, "Have mercy upon us." They really said, "Heal us."
    B. Plan—v. 28. Jesus asked the blind men if they believed He could heal them.
    C. Power—vv. 29-30
        1. Belief—v. 29. If they had faith, they could be healed. To get anything from God, we must have faith (Heb. 11:6).
        2. Blessing—v. 30. Their faith brought healing. It is your faith that brings healing.
    D. Popularity—v. 31. Jesus told the men not to tell others. Christ didn't seek popularity. However, those who were healed told others about Christ's power.

II. The perfection—32-34
    A. Possession—v. 32. A man was possessed with a devil. When Satan possesses a man, he is helpless. He can do nothing in himself. Satan controls his every move.
    B. Power—v. 33. Jesus cast out the devil, and the man was perfectly healed and restored.
    C. Persecution—v. 34. The Pharisees accused Jesus of being the prince of devils because He cast out a devil. These Pharisees didn't take into consideration that Satan cannot cast out Satan.

Strange, but when good is accomplished, the one doing the good is often criticized. At the same time, man can be sinful and wicked, yet seldom is he criticized. Why is the good man criticized? Two reasons: (1) there are many more bad people than good people; (2) the bad are convicted of their wrong, and they try to justify themselves by being critical of those who do good.

III. The preaching—vv. 35-38
    A. Preaching—v. 35. Jesus went everywhere preaching the gospel. He practiced what He preached in Mark 16:15.
    B. People—v. 36. Jesus saw the many people, and was moved with compassion, since they were lost as sheep without a shepherd (spiritual leader). How do you feel when you see the many lost souls?
    C. Problem—v. 37. There is much work to do, little time to do it in, and few workers to do it.
    D. Prayer—v. 38. Pray that God will send forth workers into the harvest of the Lord.

6 THE MASTER'S COMMISSION

Matthew 10:1-17

I. The calling—vv. 1-4
   A. The nature of the call—v. 1. Note the twofold power:
      1. Overcome unclean spirits,
      2. Overcome all sickness and disease (Mark 16:17-18). As Christians today, we have the same power.
   B. The names of those called—vv. 2-4. Their names and the meaning of the names:
      1. Simon Peter: a rock
      2. Andrew: manly, strong, brave
      3. James: deceiver
      4. John: the Lord is gracious
      5. Philip: lover of horses
      6. Bartholomew: a furrow
      7. Thomas: twin
      8. Matthew: a gift of the Lord
      9. James: son of Alphaeus
      10. Thaddaeus: praise
      11. Simon: hearing
      12. Judas: let God be praised

Matthias was chosen to fill the place of Judas who sold Christ (Acts 1:26).

II. The commission—vv. 5-16
   A. Purpose—vv. 5-6. Go to the lost sinners. We have the same call.
   B. Preaching—v. 7. Preach repentance and Christ's return.
   C. Power—v. 8. Healing and evangelizing. Give of yourself (time and energy) freely. Hold nothing back from the Lord.
   D. Provision—vv. 9-10. Step out in faith. Expect God to meet your needs. (cf. Phil. 4:19; Ps. 37:25.)
   E. Peace—vv. 11-13. God will bless those who accept God's message and God's servant.
   F. Punishment—vv. 14-15. Those who reject God and His Word will be rejected by God.
   G. Persecution—v. 16. Christians are sent as sheep among wolves. Be wise, sensible, and harmless. Be simple and sincere. Be agreeable.

III. The conflict—v. 17
   A. People will discourage you. They will try to make you give up Christ.
   B. People will denounce you. They will not encourage, but criticize you and God's work.
   C. People will degrade you. They will lie about you and will use various other methods to turn others against you.
   D. People will try to destroy you. However, God will permit them to go only so far.

Working for God is not an easy life, but God will help you and give you strength to continue.

7 JOHN THE BAPTIST AND JESUS

Matthew 11:1-19

I. **Curious people—vv. 1-3**
   A. Work of Christ—v. 1. He commanded the disciples to teach and preach in other lands.
   B. Wonder of John—vv. 2-3. John questioned whether Christ was the promised Messiah. Man need not wonder if Christ is the Messiah, for we have the complete Old Testament, which tells of the coming Messiah. It has already been proven that Christ is the Messiah, so unbelievers can only attempt to prove that He is not.

II. **Complete power—4-6**
   A. Command—v. 4. "Go and see for yourself." In other words, don't depend on others to make your decisions.
   B. Completeness—v. 5.
      1. Healing. He healed all sickness and disease.
      2. Life. The dead were raised and given life.
      3. Gospel. The gospel was preached to the poor.
   C. Consecration—v. 6. Those not ashamed of Christ were blessed.

III. **Consecrated prophet—vv. 7-14**
   A. Seeking—vv. 7-10. Jesus asked the people what they were looking for. John the Baptist was more than a prophet. Verse 10 is a quote of Malachi 3:1.
   B. Servant—v. 11. John the Baptist was chosen as God's servant. John used no fancy words, wore no fancy clothes and preached without a church building. Yet he was one of the greatest ministers of all time.
   C. Strength—v. 12. The world tries to destroy the work of God, but strong Christians can destroy the forces of evil and inherit the kingdom of God.
   D. Simplicity—vv. 13-15. John was the Elias (Elijah) of the New Testament. All Christians can be used of God in doing His work. He can provide talent for those who offer Him consecration and dedication.

IV. **Childish people—vv. 16-17**
   A. Lack of response—vv. 16-17. People did not respond to the messages of Christ. Jesus was the greatest teacher that ever lived, yet the people refused to accept His Word.
   B. Lack of respect—v. 18. Though John was a holy man sent from God, the people did not respect him. Christians should always respect their pastor as he is also sent by God.
   C. Lack of reverence—v. 19. Jesus, the Son of God came and was rejected (John 1:11).

8 REJECTION AND REST

Matthew 11:20-29

I. **The rebuke—vv. 20-24**
   A. Problem—v. 20. Christ did great work in their cities, but the people refused to repent. Though miracles were done, they rejected Christ. The same is true today.
   B. Places—vv. 21-23. Chorazin (unknown, but perhaps in northeastern Galilee); Bethsaida (see Luke 9:10); Tyre and Sidon (see 1 Kings 5:1); Capernaum in northeastern Galilee). These cities heard Christ, but refused to accept Him.
   C. Punishment—v. 24. Sodom would receive less punishment than these cities. Why? They had the full Old Testament at their disposal, whereas Sodom was destroyed before the Ten Commandments were given.

All people will be judged according to their acceptance of God's Word. Christ will be the judge. He will be fair to all men.

II. **The revelation—vv. 25-27**
   A. Secret—vv. 25-26. The things of God—spiritual concepts—are hidden from the non-Christian. One must be spiritual to understand spiritual things. Sometimes the noneducated person can understand more of God's Word than the educated person does, if the noneducated person is open to the Holy Spirit.
   B. Shown—v. 27. The Christian understands God's plan and purpose in several ways:
      1. Spirit (John 16:13). The Holy Spirit reveals spiritual things to us.
      2. Scripture (II Tim. 3:15). Studying leads to understanding.
      3. Sincerity (John 7:17). If we follow Christ, He will show us right from wrong.

Born-again Christians know God's way and Word. They have special insight into the future and are used to prepare God's kingdom.

III. **The rest—vv. 28-30**
   A. Request—v. 28.
      1. People—"Come unto me, all ye that labor and are heavy laden."
      2. Plan—"And I will give you rest." Actually this means peace and satisfaction.
   B. Rest—v. 29. Rest for the soul comes when we "take the yoke of Christ" upon us.
   C. Results—v. 30. God's way is easy compared with the way that sin and Satan offer. "Loving God means doing what He tells us to do, and that really isn't hard at all" (I John 5:3, LB).

9 PROBLEMS AND PARDON

Matthew 12:14-37

I. **The personality—vv. 14-21**
   A. Plan—vv. 14-15. The Pharisees sought how they might destroy Christ. Christ left the scene. Note, "He healed them all."
   B. Prophecy—vv. 16-21. Fulfilment of Isaiah 42:1-4. The best proof that God's Word is true is to see the fulfilled Scriptures.

II. **The power—vv. 22-23**
   A. Person—v. 22. The demon-possessed man was deaf and could not speak. This does not mean that all deaf are demon-possessed. The deaf man was healed and spoke.
   B. Prophecy—v. 23. They asked, "Is not this the son of David?" meaning, "Is not Christ the Messiah?"

The people were looking forward to the coming Messiah. As they watched Christ help and heal people, thus fulfilling Old Testament Scriptures, the people began to think, "This is Christ, the Messiah."

III. **The Person—vv. 24-30**
   A. Accusation—v. 24. Christ was accused of being the prince of devils, Beelzebub.
   B. Allegory—vv. 25-28. How could Satan cast out Satan? If Satan cast out demons he would be destroying himself. Those seeking to destroy Christ used very poor reasoning.
   C. Action—v. 29-30. Before Satan can be defeated he must be bound. Those who are not for Christ are against Him. There is no middle ground.

Sometimes when Christians are faithful in attending church, those who don't attend accuse them of "having too much religion." Others say, "He's crazy with religion." These same people never say, "He has too much sin."

IV. **The pardon—vv. 31-37**
   A. Unpardonable sin—vv. 31-32. God can forgive all sin (I John 1:7). But God cannot save a person against his will. If a person constantly rejects Christ, he is sinning against the Holy Spirit. It happened to Samson (Judg. 16:20) and Saul (I Sam. 16:14).
   B. Uncontrolled sin—vv. 33-37
      1. Sin—v. 33. We are known by our actions and speech.
      2. Speaking—vv. 34-35. We speak what is in our heart.
      3. Solemnity—vv. 36-37. We are responsible for every word we use and will be judged accordingly.

God keeps a record of all the kind words as well as the evil words we say (Ps. 19:14).

10 MEMBERS OF GOD'S FAMILY

Matthew 12:38-50

I. **The sign—vv. 38-40**
   A. Seeking—v. 38. The Pharisees sought a sign to prove Christ was the Messiah. Had they read Isaiah, they would have known He was the Messiah.
   B. Sin—v. 39. Christ told the people there would be no other sign than the sign of Jonah.
   C. Symbol—v. 40. As Jonah was in the large fish for three days, so Christ would be in the grave for three days.

II. **The Savior—vv. 41-42**
   A. Greater than man—v. 41. Christ was greater than Jonah, who in a miraculous way was freed after spending three days in the fish.
   B. Greater than kings and queens—v. 42. The queen of Sheba was great. King Solomon was one of the richest and wisest men that ever lived. Yet, Christ was greater than any person. Christ is above all (Phil. 2:9-11).

III. **The sorrow—vv. 43-45**
   Here Jesus speaks in very simple words, telling how those who once lived the Christian life went back into sin.
   A. Departure—v. 43. Satan was cast out of a man. Christians cannot be possessed by Satan; however, Satan does possess non-Christians.
   B. Degradation—vv. 44-45. Satan returned to this man's body, and the last part of his life was worse than the first.
   A person who knows Christ as Savior, but goes back into sin, is worse off than the person who never accepted Christ.

IV. **The salvation—vv. 46-50**
   A. The people—vv. 46-47. Jesus is with His mother and brothers. Nothing is said of His sisters here; however, He did have sisters (Matt. 13:55-56). Nothing is said of Joseph. Some feel he died as a young man.
   B. The picture—vv. 48-50. Jesus explained that all who do God's will are members of the family of God. What is God's will? Accepting Christ as Savior is the first step in obeying the will of God (John 1:12). God's Word reveals His will toward man. Since we are in God's family, we should share the concerns of our Christian brothers and sisters (Gal. 6:1-2).

13 TRADITION AND HOLINESS

Matthew 15:1-20

I. **The hypocrisy—vv. 1-9**
   A. Criticism—vv. 1-2. Jewish customs were added to God's law. Those who refused to keep these Jewish traditions were criticized by the rulers.
   B. Careless—v. 3. The rulers insisted that everyone keep *their* laws, but they were careless about keeping *God's* laws.
   C. Commandment—vv. 4-6. The Jews instead of helping their parents, gave the money they normally would give to their parents to the temple. (There was no Social Security then.) We should not use our tithes to help our parents although we should not neglect our parents. (I Tim. 5:8).
   D. Complaint—vv. 7-9. Prophecy of Isaiah 29:13: The people worshiped God with their lips, but their hearts were far from Him. The Jews placed their traditions and laws above the law of God.

II. **The hopelessness—vv. 10-14**
   A. Problem—v. 10. The people heard, but didn't obey. Hearing is not good enough.
   B. Practice—v. 11. "You aren't made unholy by eating non-kosher food! It is what you say and think that makes you unclean" (LB).
   C. Pharisees—vv. 12-14. The practices of the Pharisees would soon pass away. Only the teachings of Christ would endure. Man's law changes with the years, but God's Word never changes.

III. **The holiness—vv. 15-20**
   A. Parable—vv. 15-16. Peter didn't seem to understand the words of Christ: "The blind leading the blind."
   B. Practice—vv. 17-20. What you eat doesn't make you sinful. It is what comes out of your heart that is sinful. Note what comes from the heart of man.
   1. Evil and dirty thoughts. Thinking evil of others.
   2. Murder. Hating is a form of murder (1 John 3:15).
   3. Adultery. Sexual relations out of marriage by the married.
   4. Fornication. Sexual relations of the unmarried.
   5. Thefts. Taking that which does not belong to you.
   6. False witnesses. All lying is sin, regardless of how small the lie is.
   7. Blasphemies. Speaking against the Holy Spirit.
   C. Problem—v. 20. Eating without washing hands is not a sin. Ungodly works or thoughts that come out of the heart are sin.

14 CHRIST REWARDS FAITH

Matthew 15:21-31

I. The pleading faith—vv. 21-22
  A. Seeking—v. 21. Christ came to the coasts of Sidon and Tyre where people sought Him for help.
  B. Savior—v. 22. The woman called Jesus, "Lord." She knew that only Christ could cast out evil spirits. Satan works against man in these ways:
  1. Oppression—Satan constantly bothers people.
  2. Depression—Satan causes people to worry and become upset.
  3. Possession—Satan sometimes lives within people, possessing them and controlling them.

II. The persisting faith—vv. 23-27
To persist means to "keep on." We need to keep on trusting God, regardless of the circumstances.
  A. Silence—v. 23a. Jesus said nothing. Perhaps He was testing this woman's faith. Sometimes God does not answer our prayers immediately. He tests our faith. He tells us to wait.
  B. Selfishness—v. 23b. The disciples wanted to send the woman away. Perhaps they were fearful of the Gentiles. They were thinking of themselves. Who is first in your life? Christ should be first.
  C. Sheep—v. 24. Christ was not only called to Israel; He was called to help the Gentiles as well. He longs to save all people of all ages and all classes (John 3:16; Rom. 10:13; II Peter 3:9).
  D. Sincere—v. 25. She worshiped the Lord. Notice she said, "Lord help me." She saw her need and asked God for help. God cannot help us until we see our need.
  E. Scorn—v. 26. The Jews called the Gentiles "dogs." Again we see Christ testing her faith and sincerity.

III. The prevailing faith—vv. 28-31
  A. Persistence—v. 28. Because of the mother's persistence, the daughter was healed. If you have prayed and are not healed, don't give up—keeping praying.
  B. Prayer—v. 29. We see Jesus before God in prayer. We are told to take time to wait before God (Isa. 40:31).
  C. Pity—v. 30. All who were crippled were healed. Jesus not only had love; He showed love.
  D. Praise—v. 31. The people were filled with praise and wonder. If we allow Christ to work in our lives, others will be filled with praise and wonder.

15 WARNING AGAINST ERROR

Matthew 15:32-39; 16:1-12

I. The feeding—15:32-39
  A. Devotion—v. 32. The people had been with Jesus for "three days." They were hungry and had nothing to eat. Jesus loved them and couldn't send them away hungry.
  B. Doubt—v. 33. The disciples had no faith that Christ could feed all these people. They forgot how he had fed the five thousand (Matt. 14:16-21). (This is a different story, as the details prove.) Do not look upon circumstances; look to God in faith.
  C. Demand—vv. 34-35. They had seven loaves and a few fish. Jesus told the disciples to have the people sit down.
  D. Distribution—vv. 36-39. Jesus took the seven loaves and few fish, and fed four thousand men besides women and children.
God can take little and make much from it.

II. The faithless—16:1-4
  A. Seeking—vv. 1-2.
  People wanted to see miracles before they would believe. They really wanted to be entertained.
  B. Sin—v. 3. The people knew the signs of the weather, but they could not understand the signs of the times. Often the more worldly knowledge a man gains as he studies, the less he depends on God, and the less he understands about God.
  C. Sign—v. 4. Again Christ speaks of the sign of Jonah. As Jonah was in the fish for three days, so Christ would be in the grave for three days before He would arise.
The things of God are simple so that *believers* can understand, but educated *nonbelievers* stumble over them. Some try to reason with God, while others use logic. When you come to God you must accept Him by faith. You don't have to understand all things.

III. The forgetting—16:5-12
  A. The forgetting—vv. 5-6. The disciples forgot to take bread with them. As these disciples forgot to take food, many forget to take spiritual food (reading the Bible and praying daily).
  B. The faithless—vv. 7-10. They forgot how Jesus had fed the five thousand and four thousand. How easy it is to forget God's blessings! So many pray for God's blessings, then when God does bless them, they soon forget and seldom praise Him.
  C. The false followers—vv. 11-12. The Pharisees and Sadducees were teaching a false religion. Jesus warns us to be careful of these groups.

16 DIVINE PROVISION

Matthew 17:14-27

I. **The problem—vv. 14-18**
   A. Problem—vv. 14-15. This "lunatick" (epileptic) could not control himself.
   B. Powerless—v. 16. Although Christ had given the disciples the power to pray for the sick to be healed, the boy could not be cured at the time.
   C. Power—vv. 17-18. Jesus scolded the disciples for their unbelief and healed the sick boy.

II. **The power—vv. 19-21**
   A. Powerless—v. 19. The disciples were curious about their lack of power in this case.
   B. Practice—v. 20. If a man has faith the size of a mustard seed, he can move a mountain. "... Nothing shall be impossible. ..." (Also Rom. 10:17).
   C. Power—v. 21. Power to overcome Satan comes by fasting and prayer. Fasting means you will give up a meal or several meals and use the time you would normally use to eat as a time to pray.

III. **The plan—vv. 22-23**
   Three things would happen to Christ:
   A. He would be betrayed—sold by Judas.
   B. He would be crucified—nailed to the cross.
   C. He would be resurrected—rise from the grave after three days.
   Christ knew what would happen in the future. The disciples didn't comprehend the message Christ was giving.

IV. **The provision—vv. 24-27**
   A. Purpose of taxes—vv. 24-26. All Christians should be good citizens. Even if we don't agree with the government, we should pay taxes. Taxes pay for our schools, highways, and government.
   B. Provision for taxes—v. 27. Christ provided Peter with the money to pay his taxes. Peter found the money in the mouth of a fish. God provides our needs through various means.
When in need, simply call on the Lord and He will meet your needs. Don't be fearful to ask.

17 EXAMPLE FROM CHILDREN

Matthew 18:1-14

I. **The conversion—vv. 1-5**
   A. Concern—v. 1. "About that time the disciples came to Jesus to ask which of them would be the greatest in the Kingdom of heaven" (LB). This was a very selfish request.
   B. Child—v. 2. Jesus used a child to exemplify two characteristics.
      1. Tenderness—A child holds no evil feelings toward others.
      2. Teachable—A child is always open to advice and teaching.
   C. Conversion—v. 3. We must be converted and, like children, be willing to believe.
   D. Crucifixion—v. 4. Those who humble themselves will be great in the kingdom of God.
   E. Care—v. 5. "And any of you who welcomes a child like this because you are Mine, is welcoming Me and caring for Me" (LB).

II. **The complaints—vv. 6-11**
   A. Punishment—v. 6. If a person leads a child astray, causing him to lose his faith in God, God will punish him.
   B. Plan—v. 7. God's judgment will be on adults who cause children to sin. Parents will be held responsible for allowing their children to see smutty movies, to read shameful books and magazines, or to use harmful drugs.
   C. Purging—vv. 8-9. Remove that which causes you to sin. Stay away from that which would make you fall into temptation.
   D. Protection—v. 10. God has a way of protecting children, especially during their innocent years.
   E. Pardon—v. 11. Christ came to save the lost. All men who become like children may be saved.

III. **The compassion—vv. 12-14**
   A. Story—vv. 12-13
      1. The lost sheep—v. 12. The shepherd leaves the ninety-nine sheep which are safe and seeks the one that is lost.
      2. The lost soul—v. 13. God and His angels rejoice over the lost sinner who repents of his sin.
   B. Salvation—v. 14. It is not God's will that any should perish. (See His words in John 3:16; II Peter 3:9.)

18 FORGIVENESS

Matthew 18:15-35

I. **The pattern—vv. 15-22**
   A. Problem—vv. 15-17. Here is God's plan to make things right between Christians. Misunderstanding destroys God's work.
   B. Power—v. 18. Prayer power keeps Satan from hindering God's work.
   C. Prayer—v. 19. If only two people agree and join together in prayer great power is generated.
   D. Presence—v. 20. God is always present when two or three join together in the name of the Lord.
   E. Pardon—vv. 21-22. Forgive at all times as a sign of true Christianity.

II. **The practice—vv. 23-27**
   A. Parable—v. 23. Jesus gives a simple parable to explain a truth.
   B. Problem—v. 24. A man owed ten thousand talents. According to the Living Bible, this was ten million dollars.
   C. Punishment—v. 25. The king to whom the man owed the money took all the man had, including his wife and children, making them slaves.
   D. Plea—v. 26. The man asked that the king have patience with him.
   E. Pardon—v. 27. The king forgave him completely.

III. **The problem—vv. 28-30**
   A. Person—v. 28. The man who was forgiven by the king then went to a man who owed him two thousand dollars.
   B. Plea—v. 29. The man who owed the money asked for forgiveness.
   C. Problem—v. 30. Although he had been forgiven such a huge debt by the king he had no patience toward the man who owed him money.

When God forgives us, He wants us to forgive others. Yet how often we are critical toward other people. Even when God has forgiven them, we still remember their past. God forgives and forgets. We should do likewise.

IV. **The principles—vv. 31-35**
   A. Anger—vv. 31-34. The king who forgave became very angry with the servant who refused to forgive others.
   B. Attitude—v. 35. Christ will treat the unforgiving person in the same way as the king treated the unforgiving man. "The angry king sent the man to the torture chamber until he had paid every last penny due" (LB).

19 HOLINESS AND HEAVEN

Matthew 19:1-30

I. **The sacredness of marriage—vv. 1-12**
   A. Popularity—vv. 1-2. A crowd followed Jesus, and he healed them.
   B. Problem—vv. 3-6. God created man and woman for each other. They become *one* when they marry (see verse 6, ". . . not put asunder").
   C. Plan—vv. 7-8.
      1. Shame—vv. 7-8. Moses accepted divorce, but didn't approve of it. Only because of the hardness of their hearts did Moses condone divorce.
      2. Sin—v. 9. The only reason for divorce is unfaithfulness (fornication or adultery—Matt. 19:9; I Cor. 7:12-15).
   D. Practice—vv. 10-12. Some people cannot marry, and some don't want to marry. (Read these verses in the Living Bible.)

II. **The simple message—vv. 13-15**
   The kingdom of God is compared with the simplicity of a child.
   A. Children—v. 13. The disciples rebuked the parents, thinking the children were not important, but Christ blessed the children.
   B. Christ—vv. 14-15. Christ said the kingdom of heaven would be made up of people like little children. We must be simple in order to enter the kingdom of God.

III. **The salvation message—vv. 16-22**
   A. Searching—v. 16. A man asked how he might attain eternal life.
   B. Savior—vv. 17-19. Christ asked if he had kept the Ten Commandments then listed six of them.
   C. Self Righteous—v. 20. The young man said he had kept all these commands. But he was not ready for heaven, for he had not really kept the first two commandments.
   D. Sacrifice—v. 21. Being rich is not wrong, but riches kept him from God.
   E. Sorrow—v. 22. He did not want Christ's way and went away sad.

IV. **The selfish method—vv. 23-30**
   A. Salvation—vv. 23-26. It is hard for rich people to be saved since their riches so easily come between them and God. However, with God all things are possible. All men can be saved if they repent.
   B. Selfish—vv. 27-28. Peter asks what reward they would receive for following Christ. It is not what we can *get*, but what we can *give* to Christ that is important.
   C. Service—vv. 29-30. Those who serve Christ will be rewarded.

20 TEACHING AND HEALING

Matthew 20:1-34

I. **The parable—vv. 1-16**
   A. The work—vv. 1-7. A farmer hired men to work in his vineyard, paying them twenty dollars per day (LB). He hired others at 9:00 A.M., at 12 noon, at 3:00, at 4:00, and at 5:00 P.M.
   B. The wrong—vv. 8-12. Those who worked hard all day were paid the same as those who worked only a few hours. However, each one who was hired had agreed to a certain amount of money.
   C. The workers—vv. 13-16. Those who worked hard all day complained although they had agreed to twenty dollars a day. What the owner paid others was not their business. Sometimes Christians who work very hard complain about those who don't. Remember, God will take note of your work and pay you.

II. **The prophecy—vv. 17-19**
   Christ tells what would happen to Him.
   A. He would be betrayed. Judas would betray Christ for money.
   B. He would be condemned. An illegal court would condemn Christ illegally.
   C. He would be scourged. He would receive thirty-nine lashes on the back.
   D. He would be crucified. He would be nailed to the cross.
   E. He would be resurrected. After three days, He would arise from the dead.

III. **The plan—vv. 20-28**
   A. Desire—vv. 20-22. The mother of James and John wanted her two sons to sit on the right and left sides of Jesus in His kingdom.
   B. Divine—v. 23. Only God could make such a decision.
   C. Disappointment—v. 24. The other ten disciples were disappointed at their fellow disciples' selfish request.
   D. Denial—vv. 25-27. If you want to become great, deny self and do humble things; be a servant.
   E. Deliverance—v. 28. Christ is our Example. He came to serve and deliver man from his sin.

IV. **The pity—vv. 29-34**
   A. People—vv. 29-30. Two blind men sought Christ for healing.
   B. Problem—v. 31. The people tried to quiet the blind men, feeling Christ would not be interested in helping them. Christ has time for everyone. He is interested in all. He died for all.
   C. Personal—v. 32. Jesus stopped and asked the blind men their desire. He is interested in both the small and the large problems of men.
   D. Power—vv. 33-34. Jesus met the needs of the blind men by healing them.

21 FAITH AND POWER

Matthew 21:16-27

I. **The attitude—vv. 16-20**
   A. Praise—v. 16. "Yes," Jesus replied. "Didn't you ever read the scriptures? For they say, 'Even little babies shall praise Him' " (LB).
   B. Place—v. 17. They stayed in Bethany overnight.
   C. Personal—v. 18. Jesus was human, so He became hungry. He was not only the Son of God, but the Son of Man as well.
   D. Power—vv. 19-20. Christ cursed the fig tree which did not produce fruit. Note the warning of Christ to those who do not produce fruit (John 15:6).
   Christians should produce the fruits of the Spirit (Gal. 5:22-23), and should also win others to Christ.

II. **The acceptance—vv. 21-22.**
   A. Power of faith—v. 21. If we have faith and do not doubt, we can remove mountains. Faith is necessary to please God (Heb. 11:6). Faith should grow. Read Hebrews 11 to see how these great men saw wonders performed by faith.
   B. Practice of faith—v. 22. Note how we can have all things we need when we pray. The three steps are:
      1. Ask (Matt. 7:7-9).
      2. Believe (Heb. 11:1).
      3. Receive (Jer. 33:3).
   God makes it so simple for us. All we have to do is ask Him, and He will meet our needs.

III. **The authority—vv. 23-27**
   A. The concern—v. 23. The chief priests and elders asked Christ where He had received authority to do many things. They were really more critical than curious.
   B. The control—vv. 24-26. Christ was always in control. The rulers sought to trap Him many times, but He always had the correct answer. He questioned the chief priests and elders about John the Baptist's baptism. If his baptism was of heaven, why didn't they believe him? If his baptism was of men, why didn't they accept Him as a prophet?
   C. The confusion—v. 27. They could not answer. Jesus told them, "I cannot tell you by what authority I do these things." In other words, because the rulers would not answer Christ lest they convict themselves, He wouldn't answer them.

22 CHRIST IS OPPOSED

Matthew 21:28-46

I. The problem of opposition—vv. 28-32
  A. Story—vv. 28-30. One son said he wouldn't work, but later changed his mind and went to work. Another son said he would work, but didn't go.
  B. Sin—v. 31. Here Jesus says that harlots (prostitutes) and publicans (tax collectors) would enter heaven before the self-righteous Pharisees. Harlots and publicans could enter heaven because they repented.
  C. Salvation—v. 32. The self-righteous people did not accept the preaching of John the Baptist.
Good works do not produce salvation (Eph. 2:8-9). However, salvation does produce good works.

II. The persecution of opposition—vv. 33-39
  A. The parable—v. 33
    1. Winepress. Wine was made from grapes with a winepress.
    2. Tower. A watchtower was a place for the workers to stay.
    3. Let it out—*Let it out* is a phrase that means "to rent."
    4. Husbandmen. Farmers or caretakers were husbandmen.
  B. The preparation—v. 34. The owner sent servants to collect the fruit and profits from the farm.
  C. The persecution—vv. 35-38. The servants were killed.
  D. The prophecy—v. 39. This is a picture of how Christ would be rejected by mankind (cf. John 1:11-12).

III. The punishment because of opposition—vv. 40-46
  A. Story—v. 40. Here we see a comparison of what Christ will do to the wicked sinners. The wicked husbandmen were cast out. Christ will cast sinners out at the last judgment (Rev. 20:11-15).
  B. Separation—v. 41. Destruction, or separation from God. This really means hell.
  C. Stone—vv. 42-44. Jesus quoted from Psalm 118:22-23. Jesus is the stone the Jews rejected, but He became the chief cornerstone of the building.
    1. Christ the stone—v. 42. Build upon Christ and you'll have the security of a solid foundation.
    2. Producing fruit—v. 43. You must show fruit by your works.
    3. Power of the stone—v. 44. The stone will break our will, if we humble ourself. If not, the stone will fall upon us, grinding us into powder.
  D. Story understood—vv. 45-46. The people then understood His teaching and saw that Christ was referring to their own self-righteousness.

23 CHRIST AND THE WEDDING

Matthew 22:1-14

I. The invitations sent—vv. 1-7
  A. The parable—vv. 1-3. Jesus used the wedding as a parable to explain the kingdom of God. Many are invited to serve Christ, but many reject this teaching.
  B. The preparation—v. 4. A big meal was prepared for the wedding. People are invited to serve Christ as they were invited to this wedding feast, but many reject the invitation.
  C. The problem—vv. 5-6. The people who received invitations rejected them. Twice they received an invitation. Many people hear the gospel message often, but reject it.
  D. The punishment—v. 7. The king who sent the invitations sent armies to destroy those who had killed his servants (v. 6). Christ will destroy those who reject Him (Rev. 20:11-15; 21:8).

II. The invitations shunned—vv. 8-10
  A. Corrupt—v. 8. Those who were invited were not really worthy to attend. No one is worthy of salvation. We all are sinners and should die for our sins (Rom. 3:23; 6:23).
  B. Command—v. 9. Go out and compel them to come in. (See the words of Jesus in Mark 16:15; John 15:16.) Man must know he is a sinner. Unless Christians tell him, how will he know?
  C. Complete—v. 10. Both the good and bad people attend. Christ loves all people (John 3:16). He wants everyone to be saved (II Peter 3:9). He accepts all who will come (John 6:37; Rom. 10:13).

III. The indifference shown—vv. 11-14
  A. Sin—v. 11. A man was present at the wedding without a wedding garment. We need the robes of Christ's righteousness. Our own self-righteousness is as filthy rags in the sight of God (Isa. 64:6).
  B. Speechless—v. 12. The man could not answer. He really had no excuse. He knew he must have a garment. What excuse will man use when he stands before God? No excuse will be accepted by God.
  C. Sorrow—v. 13. Cast into outer darkness. Those who reject Christ will be cast into hell (Rev. 21:8).
  D. Selection—v. 14. Only those who have accepted Christ will be in heaven, and at the Marriage Supper of the Lamb.

Indifference can be one of the Christian's greatest enemies as it robs many people of the blessings of God.

24 CHRIST'S TEACHING REJECTED

Matthew 23:25-39

I. **The problem—vv. 25-26**
   A. Tradition—v. 25. They made sure the outside of the cup was clean, but inwardly they practiced:
      1. Exortion—seeking more material things and money.
      2. Excess—They lacked discipline and self-control.
   B. Teaching—v. 26. Jesus used this as an example to teach how man must be cleansed not only outwardly, but inwardly.

Tradition is practices and habits carried on through the years by man. The teachings are not given in God's Word. They are man-made laws. Anything a church teaches that doesn't agree with the Bible is wrong.

II. **The plight—vv. 27-33**
   A. Sinful—v. 27. They were outwardly holy, but inwardly they were unclean. Jesus said they were like graves full of dead bones. They had no life or reality.
   B. Stained—v. 28. They appeared to be clean, but they were stained with sin in their heart.
   C. Sinners—v. 29. The Pharisees honored the prophets who were dead, but Jesus told them that if they had lived in the days of the prophets, they too would have persecuted and killed the prophets.
   D. Sharing—v. 30. It was easy to honor the dead. These same Jewish religious leaders would later help kill Jesus.
   E. Serpents—vv. 30-33. These people would follow the path of their forefathers, who had killed the prophets. Notice how Jesus called these people "serpents."

III. **The punishment—vv. 34-39**
   A. The prophets—vv. 34-35. God sent the prophets to warn this type of people to turn from their sins. Instead of changing their way of living, however, they killed the prophets.
   B. The punishment—v. 36. God's judgment came to those who destroyed God's leaders in the past.
   C. The pity—v. 37. Jesus came and was rejected by His people. His heart was broken, because He came to help man, and man rejected His love and kindness.
   D. The peril—vv. 38-39. Jesus leaves these people alone. He does not force His love on anyone.

God does not send a person to hell—they send themselves there by their own neglect. If a person fails to accept His love, there is no other hope but for man to spend eternity in hell.

25 WAITING FOR THE KING

Matthew 25:1-13

I. The women—vv. 1-15
A. The story—v. 1. Jesus told a parable, advising us to be ready.
B. The symbols—vv. 2-4.
1. The foolish. They took no extra oil. They thought they had plenty of time to buy extra oil if they ran out.
2. The wise. They took extra oil. They were prepared. Remember, you cannot have too much of God.
C. The sleeping—v. 5. While waiting for the wedding, they all went to sleep. The wise went to sleep prepared; the foolish went unprepared.

II. The waiting—vv. 6-9
A. Preparation—vv. 6-7. The bridegroom was coming so they arose and trimmed their lamps. We must cleanse ourselves from sin, then we will be ready for His return.
B. Pleading—v. 8. The foolish asked the wise to give them some of their oil. The foolish were depending on the wise. You cannot depend on others—you must have a personal relationship with Christ yourself!
C. Personal—v. 9. The wise told the foolish to go and buy oil for themselves. You must live for God yourself—no one can do it for you. While waiting, we must keep busy for the Lord.

III. The wrong—vv. 10-12
A. The problem—v. 10. Notice these sad words, "The door was shut." The people in Noah's day had 120 years to prepare (Gen. 6:3). They refused—and the door was shut (cf. Rev. 20:11-15).
B. The plea—v. 11. "Open to us!" The door would not open for them. Today the door to heaven is open. Tomorrow it may be closed.
C. The punishment—v. 12. Notice the words, "I know you not." Only those who are born-again will enter heaven.

IV. The watching—v. 13
A. Watch your character (II Cor. 7:1). Each day we develop good or bad habits. You don't pray for good character, you develop it by daily Christian living.
B. Watch your consecration (Deut. 1:36). Here we see Caleb saying, "I wholly followed the Lord."
C. Watch your companions (II Cor. 6:17). You are known by your friends. Your friends will either help or hinder you in living for the Lord.

26 FAITHFULNESS UNTO GOD

Matthew 25:14-30

I. **The parable—vv. 14-18**
   A. Servant—v. 14. The servants met with the master before he went on a long trip. The master gave each of them money, asking that they invest it in order to make more money.
   B. Sharing—v. 15. According to the Living Bible, the amounts were: five thousand dollars, two thousand dollars, and one thousand dollars. Others were given according to their ability.
   C. Service—vv. 16-17. They put their money to work by investing it, causing it to gain interest.
   D. Shame—v. 18. The man given one thousand dollars didn't invest his money—he dug a hole and hid it in the ground. He was fearful. Many today are fearful to do anything for God, fearing what people may think and say.

II. **The people—vv. 19-25**
   A. The return—v. 19. After a long time (no exact time), the master returned. He wanted to know what had happened to the money.
   B. The results—vv. 20-23. Notice the words of praise to those who had invested their money, making it bring in interest. They were praised for their faithfulness and wisdom.
   C. The rejection—vv. 24-25. The man with one thousand dollars was fearful and hid his talent. Are you using your talent? Many have skills that could be used for God's work, but fail to use them. Therefore God's work suffers.

GOD WILL JUDGE ALL CHRISTIANS IN THESE AREAS:
1. Your time. How do you use it? Are you wasting it?
2. Your money. Do you tithe? Does God come first in money matters? Are you willing to sacrifice?
3. Your abilities and skills. Are you using them wisely? Are you doing all you can?

III. **The punishment—vv. 26-30**
   A. Laziness—v. 26. "But his master replied, wicked man! Lazy slave! Since you knew I would demand your profit. . ." (LB).
   B. Loss—vv. 27-30. This man's talent was taken from him and given to the person who made his five thousand dollars increase to ten thousand dollars and the foolish man was cast into outer darkness. Because of his indifference and unwise acts he was not accepted.
   C. Learn—God's judgment will come to all people (Heb. 9:23, II Cor. 5:10, Rev. 20:11-15).